# Dat

MW00977701

# Destiny

*Making Right choices.*

To. Joseph Njenga.

Anganga

05/31/2015

May this book guide you
make right choices and
have a reason to
live & see tomorrow!

## A Reflection on the Life of Lot
## Rev. Antony Kimani Nganga
*Forewarded by* Dr. Christopher S. Bowen

Rev Antony Kimani Nganga

Printed in the United States of America

Published by:

CreateSpace Independent Publishing Platform

ISBN-13: 978-1502354549

ISBN-10: 1502354543

Rev Antony Kimani Nganga

## DEDICATION

My Dad Mr. Samuel Nganga, who calls me 'my beloved son' and shaped my life, dreams, and shaped my character.

My Mum Mrs. Grace Njoki Nganga, who believed in the beauty of my dreams. You invested your time and all you had to ignite and nurture my dreams.

My Brother Paul Njuguna, a man of passion and ability. Your sense of humor is remarkable!

My sister Lilian Njeri, who loves me unconditionally. You are a special gift in our family.

Rev Antony Kimani Nganga

## ACKNOWLEDGEMENTS

I would like to thank my mentor Dr. Christopher Scott Bowen. He read the first manuscript of this book and donated his laptop after recognizing my passion in writing. Above all, I want to thank my family who supported and encouraged me in spite of all the time it took me away from them. It was a long and difficult journey for them.

I would like to thank Dr. Benson Karanja, the President Beulah Heights University in Atlanta GA, and Dr. Sam Chand, who both worked behind the scenes in making my dreams come true. May your fountain be blessed!

Rev Jim Kimotho, the Director African Growth Ministries. You ignited passion to chase my dreams and awakened the sleeping giant in me. You are my cheerleader!

Thanks to Apostle David Karanja & Pst Teresia Karanja, founders of Christ Harvesters Church in Marietta GA USA. They took me like their own son and sacrificed their resources. You are part

Rev Antony Kimani Nganga
of my success story! Your warmth, generous spirit, and compassion will be missed forever.

Pastor Daniel Ndung'u, my Dad in the diaspora. May the Lord will reward you for your generosity and kindness. You are a true servant!

The Rev. Richard Mungai and family of Restoration Assemblies International in Acworth, GA USA. You believed and prophesied greater things in my life. Martin Wairimu, Elizabeth Mweru, Sylvia Kirechu, Isaac Kariuki, Mr & Mrs Leonard Gichaga, and Forever young group in Marietta GA. You remain a blessing in my life!

Last, but not the least: I beg forgiveness of all those who have been with me over the course of the years and whose names I have failed to mention.

## FOREWORD

It is truly amazing how God brings people into our lives to teach us valuable lessons. Antony Kimani is one of those people! As a full-time Professor at Beulah Heights University, I have been blessed to meet many international students. Mr. Kimani is one that will leave a lasting impression long after his studies here are done. He reminds us of God's faithfulness to His promises. When God calls us into the ministry, it's not up to us to figure out how, when, why and where. We are simply to obey His voice. Antony's testimony is that he did just that.

When God told him to leave his country and come to Atlanta, Georgia to attend the University, he trusted that God would provide for his every need. He didn't hesitate. He knew he had a destiny to fulfill.

In his book, *Date with Destiny,* Mr. Kimani reflects on the biblical lessons we find in the story of Lot, his family, and how the choices they made affected their lives. You will be blessed as you read

Rev Antony Kimani Nganga

this book, and you will be inspired to count the cost of the decisions you make in your personal life.

The only thing that can hinder you from the future God has for you is YOU. Just as Mr. Kimani has taught us all, we have a date with destiny! Be determined to reach yours!

Dr. Christopher S. Bowen
Founder & Overseer,
Living Faith Int'l Ministries
Forest Park, Georgia
USA

# Contents

Rev Antony Kimani Nganga

# 1

# Understanding

# Destiny

Rev Antony Kimani Nganga

## 1

## Understanding Destiny

*"It is not in the stars to hold our destiny but in ourselves."*

— *William Shakespeare*—

A layman's understanding of destiny may be the events that will necessarily happen to a particular person or thing in the future.

Destiny may also be understood as the predetermined course of events considered as something beyond human power or control. Most Christians subscribe to this school of thought in relation to destiny.

It is simple but difficult to define destiny as a concept. However, there are different approaches and schools of thought employed in search for the answer. But it's not only complex but also challenging to unravel the definition. This is because the definition will be limited to someone's exposure and worldview.

First, some people have an exalted view of it. Secondly, its nature raises unanswerable questions about the events in the future. Moreover, Christians subscribes to different beliefs and traditions in their concept of destiny.

> "The only person you are destined to become is the person you decide to be."
> *Ralph Waldo Emerson*

Finally, Scholars and philosophers also differ in their definitions.

The Bible is the clear guide for Christians to understand the concept of destiny as it relates to eternity. The scripture exemplifies the will of God to man from the beginning to eternity. *'For in him we live, and move, and have our being'* Acts 17:28 (KJV). Our destiny is assured by the fact that Christ died on the cross to redeem mankind (John 3:16)

There are two things that will help us understand our destiny. They are: -

a) Purpose

b) Persistence & Perseverance


### a) Purpose

*"If you can't figure out your purpose, figure out your passion. For your passion will lead you right into your purpose"*

*Bishop TD Jakes*

Purpose is simply the reason why you were created. Many people live a life of experiments for they don't know their purpose on earth. For you to understand your destiny, you must know why God created you. Nobody is born knowing their purpose in life. Purpose is discovered not achieved!

Apostle Paul said *'And we know that for those who love God all things work together for good, for those who are called according to his purpose.'* (Romans 8:28 ESV).

The verse is a motivation for our souls in the midst of trials and sufferings. As long as God has called me according to his purpose, nothing can stop me from living to fulfill that purpose!

Purpose is God's action plan that moves us from where we are to the place He wants us to be. We can only discover our purpose, when we allow our will to be lost in the will of God. Paul reminds us in Romans 12:2, *'Do not be conformed to this world, but be transformed by the renewal of your mind, that by testing you may discern what is the will of God, what is good and acceptable and perfect* (ESV).

> "Sometimes the dreams that come true are the dreams you never even knew you had."
>
> *Alice Seybold, the Lovely Bones*

Therefore, we may infer from the Apostle Paul and say that it's the renewed mind that is able to discern the will of God. One is able to know where God is taking them by committing their will to Him. It is by doing this fact, that God directs our steps in our life as evidenced by King David in Psalms 119:105.

> "There is no greater gift you can give or receive than to honor your own calling. It's why you were born. And how you become most truly alive"
>
> *Oprah Winfrey*

We can understand our destiny by seeing ourselves through the eyes of God. He told the prophet Jeremiah *"Before I formed you in the womb I knew you, and before you were born I consecrated you; I appointed you a prophet to the nations."* (Jer. 1:5 ESV) Jeremiah gained confidence by seeing himself as a change agent in the society for walking on the promises of God. Actually, this is what happens when you understand God's plan for your life.

The time I realized divine anointing over my life as a minister of the Gospel, I didn't go to ask the Bishop(s) for confirmation. I started doing His will in relation to my calling. Nobody can understand the anointing in your life unless it's revealed to them by the Lord. It's neither your businesses nor their business to prove the same. It's the Lord's business!

The big question God will ask me is 'what did you do with what I entrusted you?' The reason why Paul told Timothy *"[20] O Timothy, guard the deposit entrusted to you. Avoid the irreverent babble and contradictions of what is falsely called "knowledge,"* (1 Tim 6:20 ESV)

Purpose is the reason you up in the morning and believe you will succeed in the midst of overwhelming challenges. It's the unstoppable inward strength that ignites passion in the life of an individual. It's a constant reminder of a better tomorrow for greater expectations.

*"To be able to get out of bed and do what you love for the rest of the day is beyond words."* - **John Schroeder**

Nothing that has the ability to nullify one's purpose in life. But the task to is turning purpose into reality. That's the ultimate truth! Writer Richard Bach says, *"You're never given a wish without also being given the power to make it true. You may have to work for it, however."* The purpose conceived in one's life will never exist, without the power to make it come true and bearable.

> "Keep your dreams alive. Understand to achieve anything requires faith and belief in yourself, vision, hard work, determination, and dedication. Remember all things are possible for those who believe".
>
> - **Gail Devers**

## b) Persistence & perseverance

*"Ambition is the path to success. Persistence is the vehicle you arrive in."*

### Bill Bradley

Persistence is simply making a firm decision to accomplish a task in life in spite of, difficulty or opposition. It's flowing against the currents to achieve your goals in life. Persistence wears out resistance!

Dennis Whitley once said, "As long as we are persistence in our pursuit of our deepest destiny, we will continue to grow. We cannot choose the day or time when we will fully bloom. It happens in its own time." It's being persistent that keeps a believer moving on in the midst of obstacles. Persistence develops perseverance in our lives. Although these words are used interchangeably in the modern world. Paul Said in Romans 5:3 that *'we also exult in our tribulations, knowing that tribulation brings about perseverance;'* (NASB)

> "It's not that I'm so smart, it's just that I stay with problems longer."
>
> *Albert Einstein*

The word 'tribulation' is derived from a Greek word *'thlipsis'* which has the same meaning as oppression, distress, affliction, and tribulation. But it's going through troubles in life that brings out perseverance. In other words, our sufferings act as the industry that produces perseverance. Perseverance is the resulting product!

Therefore, we have to endure sufferings with an attitude of being in God's potter's house. This is how God molds our character that eventually shapes our destiny. Isaiah tells us in Isaiah 55:8 that *"For my thoughts are not your thoughts, neither are your ways my ways," declares the LORD* (NIV).

According to the Gospel of John 16:33, *'These things I have spoken unto you, that in me ye might have peace. In the world ye shall have tribulation: but be of good cheer; I have overcome the world.'* (KJV)

He gives an assurance and hope when going through sufferings. The word 'peace' mentioned in this verse is not the word 'peace' found in Mt 10:13 where Jesus held his peace. Jesus was telling his disciples to have the tranquil state of a soul assured of it's salvation through Him, and so fearing nothing from God and content with it's earthly Lot, of whatsoever that lot is. He just wanted them to have the blessed state of devout and upright men after death.

Jesus desire was to help the disciples understand their destiny. He had to assure them that all they needed is His peace which is beyond Oxford learners' dictionary definition.

> "If you can't fly then run, if you can't run then walk, if you can't walk then crawl, but whatever you do you have to keep moving forward."
> *Martin Luther King Jr.*

# 2

# Muslim Concept of

# Destiny

Rev Antony Kimani Nganga

### 2

## Muslims belief of Destiny

Islam is the current predominant religion of all Arab countries and parts of Africa. They believe salvation is dependent on man and not God. That's why they devote themselves in reading the Muslim Bible 'Koran' to learn the doctrine revealed by Muhammad.

"The heart of human excellence often begins to beat when you discover a pursuit that absorbs you, frees you, challenges you, or gives you a sense of meaning, joy, or passion"

*Terry Orlick*

Muslims believe in *Allah* who is the creator of all things, including their actions. *Allah,* is in control of their destiny and they have very little or nothing to do about it.

The *Qadar,* simply translated as Divine destiny, is one of their six articles of faith. *Qadar* expresses that one has the freedom, the choice, to do as he/she wants and have no control of those choices. Their destiny is the product of their choices, and only *Allah* who knows what that destiny is.

To reinforce this, we will have a closer look at some verses in the Holy Quran. One of the articles in Quran, al-Anam, 6:59 states *"With Allah are the keys of the Unseen, the treasures that none knows but Allah; ...and there falls not a leaf but Allah knows it, nor a grain in the darkness of the earth nor anything green nor dry but (it is all) in a clear book."*

Also, Surah ar-Rad, 13:8 states *"Allah knows what every female bears, and that of which the wombs fall short of completion and that in which they increase; and there is a measure with Allah of everything."*

These verses and many similar verses declare that everything was, in the knowledge of God before they were created. Its opposite cannot be thought because the knowledge of God surrounds everything, every time and every place. Not accepting it means attributing ignorance to God. However, far is God from all faults and defects.

If a destiny for man did not exist and if God knew man's actions after the event happened, an end and a limit would have come to the knowledge of God and an increase, a decrease and a change would have been in question. However, none of them can be thought about God.

> "I do not feel obliged to believe that same God who endowed us with sense, reason, and intellect had intended for us to forgo their use."
> -*Galileo*

As we will also mention in the issue of being eternal, the knowledge of God surrounds everything. Namely, all creatures; past, present, future, earlier, last, external, internal, secret, evident... Shortly, everything is in God's circle of observation in every moment.

Nothing can be hidden from the knowledge of God. Consequently, if we say that there is no destiny for man, it means God does not know tomorrow because if God knows tomorrow, for every man there will be a destiny because destiny is the title of divine knowledge. In short, there is a destiny and it is real.

Christian faith is not merely faith based on works, but on the redeeming work of Christ on the cross. Therefore, we have a responsibility of working out our own salvation with fear and trembling in accordance to the leading of the Holy Spirit. (Phil 2:12). This concept takes us back to the cross where Christ died as a ransom for many for the forgiveness of sins. Therefore, our destiny is both assured and eternal (John 3:16; 36, 1 Jn. 4:9)

# 3

# Biblical Concept of

# Destiny

Rev Antony Kimani Nganga

**3**

**Biblical Concept of Destiny**

*'There is a higher power, a higher influence, a God who rules and reigns and controls circumstances and situations that are beyond your area and realm of authority'*

*-Bishop TD Jakes -*

Destiny doesn't originate from within us, neither is it generated by our desires or ideas. Our destiny originates in the mind of God (Jer. 1:5, Act17:28). This is evident in the Hebrew canon as we focus on the man Moses. He lived for forty years in the desert, and had an encounter with God at the burning bush. It was here that God was very clear of what He wanted Moses to do. It was now up to Moses to heed to his destiny or reject it by obeying the Lord's voice (Ex. 3).

God's sovereignty does not undo human responsibility. Even if God is good, compassionate, loving and forgiving, we are responsible for our actions. God made stone with the characteristics of being hard, and so it is. He made waters with the characteristics of being wet, and so it is. He also created man with the ability of being responsible for his choices.

We are all responsible of the choices we make every moment. The Bible is full of persons that faced the consequences of their actions, which influenced their destiny either positively or negatively. When God created Adam and Eve, He placed them in the Garden of Eden (Gen 1:27), and gave them instructions. They were to live by those instructions. Instead, they chose to disobey voluntarily against the promptings of God who lived with them and was greater than Satan. This affected the destiny of man since then!

> "Destiny is a name often given in retrospect to choices that had dramatic consequences."
>
> *J.K. Rowling*

But God in His sovereignty, had a foreordained plan of reconciling man back to Himself. The incarnation of Jesus Christ in the New Testament was the plan to redeem mankind. The Holy Spirit in this dispensation is in operation in the lives of his people.

"What is the point of having free will if one cannot occasionally spit in the eye of destiny?"
*Jim Butcher,*
*White Night*

The patriarch Abraham is an example of how God walks with individuals who are fully committed to obey his decrees. Genesis 17 says, *'When Abram was ninety-nine years old, the* LORD *appeared to him and said, "I am God Almighty: walk before me faithfully and be blameless.* [2] *Then I will make my covenant between me and you and will greatly increase your numbers."* (NIV). *God* was expecting Abraham to remain committed to him by following divine decrees so as to realize his destiny. As a result, Abraham was blessed and became very wealthy in livestock and in silver and gold (Gen 13:2), for he followed God's instructions.

Lot is a biblical figure that portrays how the fallen nature can interfere with Divine guidance. In anthropology, Biblical Scholars suggests that the old man is in a comma. This implies that God can call a person to be a preacher, but the person can kill the preacher God called.

Lot heard the instructions from the angels and yet chose to follow his finite mind contrary to the infinite will of God. Since our God is not a dictator, He allowed him to make choices and was held accountable for his actions. We can be assured of our destiny, if we allow God to guide us every moment.

> "There's never an age when you are too young to make a difference in some way."
> **Antony Kimani**

Therefore, this is an arena that must ever remain as an affair of religion rather than of science. In other words, it must remain one of that class of questions upon which I may not expect to convince my neighbor, while at the same time I may entertain a reasonable conviction of my own upon the subject.

Rev Antony Kimani Nganga

# 4.

# The Sodom Experience

Rev Antony Kimani Nganga

**4**

## The Sodom experience

(Gen 19:1-15).

*"Some men are born sodomites, some achieve sodomy, and some have sodomy thrust upon them..."*

*Aleister Crowley*

The word Sodom is derived from the Hebrew word *'sedom'* which means burning. According to the Hebrew canon, the kingdoms of Sodom and Gomorrah were allied with the cities of Admah, Zeboim and Bela. These five cities, also known as the "cities of the plain", they were situated on the Jordan River plain in the southern region of the land of Canaan. The plain, which corresponds to the area just north of the modern-day Dead Sea, was compared in Genesis 3:10 with the Garden of Eden as being a land well-watered and green, suitable for grazing livestock.

The common reason why Lot lived in Sodom was to manage his own riches. They had prospered in the land of Canaan. We are told in Genesis 13:1-9 that, the land could no longer support the flocks of Abram and Lot together. He had to make a decision that would propel his goals in life like many of us. Lot lived in a land which gave him satisfaction economically, but the land was wicked. Genesis 13:13, says that *'Now the men of Sodom were wicked and sinners against the LORD exceedingly'*. The land was good; its inhabitants, however, left much to be desired. Lot's decision would cost him greatly! Let us now consider the consequences of Lot's decision to live in the midst of an exceedingly wicked people.

> "I believe purpose is something for which one is responsible; it's not just divinely assigned"
>
> *Michael Fox*

Lot was not the only one to see that the land was good; it was also under the hand of kings from the east. These kings fought against the kings of the area of Sodom, defeated them, and Lot was taken captive (Gen 14:1-12). Had it not been for Abram and his forces, Lot would have lost everything and would have been a slave back in Mesopotamia (Genesis 14:13-16)! Later, when Lot received divine visitors as guests, he felt compelled to offer the Sodomites his own daughters to defile rather than the visitors (Genesis 19:1-8).

The next day, Lot fled from Sodom as God rained fire and brimstone upon the city, and his wife turned into a pillar of salt when she looked back (cf. Genesis 19:17-29). While his wife made the decision by herself to look back

> "You can't just sit there and wait for people to give you that golden dream, you've got to get out there and make it happen for yourself"
>
> *Dianna Ross*

and disobey God, had Lot never been in Sodom in the first place, the temptation would not have been present!

Despite the fact that Lot was a righteous man, He lived in Sodom. He was familiar with every evil practices of the region. The evil environment had a negative impact in His moral and spiritual beliefs. This analogy speaks volumes to us today!

The environment we choose to live can contaminate with what we claim to stand for as believers. There's a series of events in Lots life that support this fact. He chose for himself Sodom that challenged his faith. He also chose Zoar but still felt to move in the cave.

"If you organize your life around your passion, you can turn your passion into your story and then turn your story into something bigger – something that matters"

*Blake Mycoskie*

The cave environment was a fertile ground for evil. Lot was simply looking for a comfort zone which was contrary to the divine plan of God. This is what happens when we decide to lead ourselves; evil has a way of catching with us. We must clothe ourselves '*with the full armor of God so that you may be able to stand against the schemes of the devil*' (Eph. 6:11 NET)

The ability for Lot making the right decision to move out of Sodom was compromised by staying in Sodom. Our worldview and decisions are greatly influenced and shaped by the environment exposed to us. Christian faith has never been in a vacuum but in a cultural environment that has values, customs and beliefs. We should acknowledge that, we are in the world and not of the world as Apostle Paul wrote in Rom 12:2, 1 John

> "Our destiny changes with our thought; we shall become what we wish to become, do what we wish to do, when our habitual thought corresponds with our desire.
>
> *Orison Swett Marden*

2:15. Therefore, surrounding our lives with people who have a positive impact and ignite the love of God in our hearts is rewarding and great gain.

Lot's ability to raise good children was compromised by his series of choices. Lot's daughters were married to certain men of the city; while we do not know how righteous they were, we know that there were fewer than ten in the whole city, and therefore it is doubtful that they were good influences (cf. Gen18:31-33)

Jesus spoke in Matt 5:13 by proclaiming *'Ye are the salt of the earth: but if the salt have lost his savor, wherewith shall it be salted? it is thenceforth good for nothing, but to be cast out, and to be trodden under foot of men.'* Writer, pastor, and leadership coach, Dr. Sam Chand once said, '…we are like a tea bag'. A tea bag changes water into a tea. The same way a tea bag influences the color of water, so are we to influence the lost world into the kingdom of God. A tea bag reminds us the power of being a change agent. The power to transform the world in and out of season.

*"One secret of success in life is for a man to be ready for his opportunity when it comes."*

~ *Benjamin Disraeli*

Rev Antony Kimani Nganga

# 5

# The Cave

# Exposure

Rev Antony Kimani Nganga

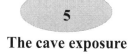

## The cave exposure

*'Exceptionally hard decisions can deplete your energy, to the point at which you cave in. If you mentally crumble and degenerate into negative thinking, you will magnify the problem where it can haunt you'.*

### John C. Maxwell

### Gen 19:31 -32 (NET)

*Later the older daughter said to the younger, "Our father is old, and there is no man anywhere nearby to have sexual relations with us, according to the way of all the world.*

*³²Come, let us make our father drunk with wine so we can have sexual relations with him and preserve our family line through our father.*

The word exposure is commonly used in photography and film industry. The web dictionary defines exposure as the revelation of an identity or fact. Other synonymous words include; uncovering, disclosure, unmasking and discovering.

Eventually, lot ended up in the cave with his two daughters. It's in the cave that his own daughters devised a plan and made their father drunk with wine, in order to secure their generation. However, the cave was a fertile ground for evil and not for godly activities. But God who is both immanent and transcendent was very present in the cave.

In the Hebrew canon, there are two common known caves among others. They include: - the cave Of Adullam (1Sam 22:1; 2Sam 23:13; 1Chr 11:15). And the cave of En-Gedi (1Sam 24:3-8). These caves served as a place of refuge (Josh 10:16-27; Judg 6:2; 1Sam 13:6; 1Kgs 18:4; 1Kgs 18:13; 1Kgs 19:9; 1Kgs 19:13), or as a burial place (Gen 23:9-20; Gen 25:9; Gen 49:29-32; Gen 50:13; John 11:38)

Furthermore, the fact that they both made their father drunk so as to have children by him, does not speak well of them (Genesis 19:30-38). Since Sodom was so saturated with sin, should we be surprised to consider that Lot's daughters were easily infected by it?

> "One meets his destiny often in the road he takes to avoid it."
>
> *French Proverb*

While we cannot know what was going through Lot's mind while he was in the cave after the destruction of Sodom, we can wonder whether he was reflecting back on that fateful day recorded in Genesis 13 when he made his decision to pitch his tents toward Sodom. If he had to do it all over again, what choice would he have made?

Rev Antony Kimani Nganga

We can certainly sympathize with Lot's plight, for we ourselves live in a sinful world and have been called to live in the midst of sinners (1 John 2:15-17, 1 Corinthians 5:9-10). It is not as if we have the opportunity to separate ourselves entirely from sinners; how can we be lights in darkness if we are only around the light? (cf. Matthew 5:13-16)

Nevertheless, many times we do have the opportunity to make decisions as to where we will live, and we ought to consider Lot's example when we do. After all, Abraham also lived as a sojourner in the midst of people who also were sinners, and yet he did not suffer nearly as much as Lot! The land was perhaps not as good in the rest of Canaan, but the people were not as exceedingly sinful and respected Abraham (cf. Gen 23:3-6).

The daughters of Lot made a wise decision out of a frustration. It wasn't their choice to live in the cave, but their father took them there and were expected to make choices even in that environment.

Their choice as evident in the Hebrew canon, was not only based on lust but on future as well. '….so we can preserve our family line through our father (Gen 19:34 NET). Sometimes God allows us to go through some crisis so as to think beyond the situation and understand His divine purpose for our lives.

Today, most of us go through crisis but rarely see Christ in the crisis. It's only when we'll start thinking different during frustrating moments our situations will change. We cannot expect a situation to change, if we are doing nothing about it.

"You are what your deep driving desire is;

As your deep driving desire is, so is your will;
As your will is so is your deed;
As your deed is so is your destiny.

*Maitri Upanishads*

Like the daughters of Lot, most of us have made decisions based on our situations. We ended up suffering as a consequence of our choices. It doesn't necessarily mean because you are suffering, you made the wrong decisions. People suffer for different reasons. There are some people who are suffering because of their sins. There are others who are suffering simply because God is moving them to another level.

As long as God is involved in it, and the motive of doing it is right, keep on doing it until something happens. Many are afraid of rising up for fear of 'what people will say' syndrome. Such folks need to know that God did not create us to be nice, but to be effective! Keep on pressing on and let nothing stop you from achieving your goals in life.

Others under-utilize their gifts due to frustration. God simply uses what you have. The Lord asked Moses *""What is that in your hand?" A staff," he* replied (Ex 4:2). It was through this rod that he was able to perform miraculous signs (Ex 4:17). What do you have in your hands? God uses what you have to accomplish his divine plans.

He sees what everybody else ignores. I have met people who full of excuses on how they can't make a positive difference in their lives based on their past experiences and failures. It doesn't matter how young or old you are – you can still make a difference in your world today. There's never an age when you are too young to make a difference in some way. If you have a cause or an idea you are passionate about, take a step of courage and start doing it right away.

> "Sow a thought and you reap an act;
> Sow an act and you reap a habit;
> Sow a habit and you reap a character;
> Sow a character and you reap a destiny."
>
> *Ralph Waldo Emerson*

We may be called upon to choose between two habitations. One may represent a great financial opportunity, and one will easily be able to satisfy physical needs and to support the family. What if that place has no congregation of brethren of like precious faith? With whom will you associate? How will you teach your children righteousness? There may be another habitation, where one will perhaps not have the best opportunity, but one can associate with good brethren and at least gain the respect of the rest of the community. Is it not the benefit to the family far more worthwhile than a bit more money?

The cave exposure is not and will never be the mountain exposure. It's hard for those who have once lived on the mountain to start living in the cave. We can't consult those that have been on the cave about the mountain experience because they have nothing to tell. However, it's difficult for those who have been in the cave to take us to the mountain. The advice to the mountain, can only be from those who have experienced the mountain. They understand the temperatures, humidity, and a different visual view which can't be experienced in the cave.

It's the responsibility of every individual to consider seeking advice from the right persons. You can't consult the cave exposed folks about the mountain experience! Though the cave was under the mountain, I suggest that Lot would had a different worldview if only he had time to climb and experience the mountain.

It seems the daughters of Lot were going around the mountain (Gen. 19: 31) but they didn't experience the mountain. Exposure is what brings all the difference!

We can relate this today with our relationship to God. We can experience the church of God and fail to relate with the God of the church.

Most folks are motivated in serving the program of God without having a relationship with the God of the program. God is interested in having a personal relationship with him.

God has placed us on earth and we can choose to live on the mountain or in the cave. But His desire is for us to live on the mountain and experience Him at a personal level.

Rev Antony Kimani Nganga

Many are the times we put boundaries to the extent we think our gifts can operate. Mostly, we do this by considering our level of exposure. The challenge with this is that we limit our potential of doing the extra-ordinary in the world of God.

When exposed, you can know where to go, with who and when. A choice of where one needs to go is in direct consideration with who you want to go with. Failure to consider the above factors, will lead us in the wrong places, doing the wrong things and with the wrong people.

> "As long as we are persistent in our pursuit of our deepest destiny, we will continue to grow. We cannot choose the day or time when we will fully bloom. It happens in its own time."
>
> *Denis Waitley*

# 6

# God in

# our

# limitations

Rev Antony Kimani Nganga

**6**

## God in our Limitations

*'There are three methods to gaining wisdom. The first is reflection, which is the highest. The second is limitation, which is the easiest. The third is experience, which is the bitterest'.*

### *- Confucius –*

Limitation is inability or lack of capacity to achieve one's goals in life. It's true that, have flaws and imperfections: physical, emotional, mental and spiritual. It is true that all of us have limitations in our lives, but very few that recognizes human limitation as divine visitation.

His Excellency, Hon Uhuru Kenyatta, the fourth President of the Republic of Kenya asked a question, "Who doesn't have limitations?" He further pointed out that, having limitations is not the problem. The problem is when we fail to recognize those limitations as opportunities to do better.

Rev Antony Kimani Nganga

The inability to accomplish our goals in life does not necessarily reflect God's inability to work it out for us. Actually, human limitation is directly proportional to the divine invitation! Limitations are the catalyst that speeds up the rate of seeking God in our lives.

The word Lot comes from the root word 'veil' which is the same as 'covering' in the King James Version of the Bible. Lot lived to the very nature of his name as evident with the choices he made in his life and the cave drama with his two daughters.

He indeed acted like as a man whose mind was covered and gullible. He finally ended up in the cave with his two daughters that gave him wine and eventually slept with him. His first daughter gave birth to Moab, who is the ancestor of Moabites today.

> "Control your destiny or somebody else will."
>
> - *Jack Welch*

The second born gave birth to Ben-Ammi (Ammonites).

In the generation of genealogy of Jesus

Christ as recorded by the Gospel according to Matthew c.f Mtt.1:1-14 you will not see Leah or Rachael. But Rehab who was a Harlot, is included in the genealogy, you will also see Bathsheba, the wife of Uriah who committed adultery with David. This teaches us that Christ didn't only come to save sinners, but in His lineage there are sinners. God's divine plan of the messiah was fulfilled through the lineage of sinners.

God does not depend on our choices for His eternal plans to prevail. Moreover, there is nothing we can do to nullify God's foreordained plans. God is never left out in the equation when we make choices.

It is through limitation that our faith is developed. Faith will never grow without problems, trials and hardships. When a believer asks God for more faith, that person is asking for an increased burden. Unshakable faith comes from having your faith shaken.

Apostle Paul, in the Bible had a thorn in the flesh as his limitation. In 2 Cor. 12:7 (NIV) says, *6 For even if I wish to boast, I will not be a fool, for I would be telling the truth, but I refrain from this so that no one may regard me beyond what he sees in me or what he hears from me, 7 even because of the extraordinary character of the revelations. Therefore, so that I would not become arrogant, a thorn in the flesh was given to me, a messenger of Satan to trouble me – so that I would not become arrogant. 8 I asked the Lord three times about this, that it would depart from me. 9 But he said to me, "My grace is enough for you, for my power is made perfect in weakness." So then, I will boast most gladly about my weaknesses, so that the power of Christ may reside in me. 10 Therefore, I am content with weaknesses, with insults, with troubles, with persecutions and difficulties for the sake of Christ, for whenever I am weak, then I am strong.*

> "It is in your moments of decision that your destiny is shaped."
> *Anthony Robbins*

Weaknesses are not accidents. God deliberately allows them in our life for the purpose of demonstrating His power through us. God has never been impressed with strength and self-sufficiency. The Bible is filled with examples of how God loves to use imperfect, people to do extraordinary things in spite of their weakness.

A limitation is not a sin or a vice or a defect that we can change like overeating and impatience. This limitation is inherited and we have no power to change. It may be a physical limitation like trauma, hurt memory, and intellectual limitation.

When we think of limitations in our life we may be tempted to conclude, "God could never use me." Let us remember that God is beyond and above limits. In fact, He enjoys putting His great power into ordinary "containers". *"We are like clay jars in which this treasure is stored. The real power comes from God and not from us."* (2 Corinthians 4:7). Like common pottery, we are fragile and flawed. We may break easily but God will use us if only we allow

When I was growing up, my dream was to be like Beethoven. I loved his music so much. Little did I know that he was deaf! Franklin D. Roosevelt is said to have been the most powerful president of the United States, yet he ruled for four terms from a wheelchair. Milton was blind yet, he was among the best poetry writers in the world. God is always involved in our limitations with a purpose of unleashing our potential.

God calls the unqualified and qualifies them. Apostle Paul in 1 Cor. 1:27 says *"But God chose the nonsense in*

"How a person masters his fate is more important than what his fate is."

*- Karl Wilhelm von Humboldt*

*the world to make the wise feel ashamed. God chose what is weak in the world to make the strong feel ashamed"* (ISV). God is never misplaced from our limitations. In fact, our limitations are God's invitation in our life.

Am encouraged by Jabez in 1Chronicles 4:10, when he refused to live by the standards and description(s) of his name! The meaning of the word 'Jabez' means pain. He prayed for blessings upon his life and God granted his request.

> "We may become the makers of our fate when we have ceased to pose as its prophets."
> - *Sir Karl Popper*

You can rise above your limitations and walk to your ordained destiny. It only takes the 'Jabez' kind of believers who will proclaim and see greater things ahead. I've not only heard greater but I've seen God does in the business of doing greater things.

We are responsible of what happens in our lives as we make choices that create the future. We often find it easy to blame others for whatever goes in our lives.

Often, we believe we are victims of circumstance. We blame our grandparents for inheriting their genes. We blame our parents for shaping our childhood experiences. Our teachers for assigning us poor grades. Even the government for taking all the money through tax. Despite all of the above, we are still left to make choices and recognize that God is involved in bringing out His divine plan.

# 7

# What

# Limits Your

# Potential?

Rev Antony Kimani Nganga

**What limits your potential?**

*"One of the greatest tragedies in life is to watch potential die untapped."*

\_\_\_\_*Myles Munroe*\_\_\_\_

In ancient biblical times, caves mostly served either as cemetery c.f Gen 25:19 or a hiding place c.f Gen 49:30, Jos 10:16. In 1 Samuel 22, we see David hiding from King Saul at the Cave of Adullam. But David unlike Lot and his two daughters saw it as an opportunity that would draw him closer to God. David wrote Psalms 57 in this cave which demonstrated his spiritual focus, strength and growth. This is a practical

> The will to win, the desire to succeed, the urge to reach your full potential... these are the keys that will unlock the door to personal excellence.
>
> *Confucius*

demonstration that a cave can be a spring of revival when one remains focused unto God.

In the cave, we can encounter God or the devil. After David had encountered God in the cave, he didn't revenge for himself. The cave was a place to wait upon the Lord. We are told in 1 Sam 24 verse 3, that '*Saul came to the sheepcotes by the way, where was a cave; and Saul went in to cover his feet: and David and his men remained in the sides of the cave*' (KJV). David knew that Saul was searching after his life, but David allowed God to fight his battles. This is what happens when we hide in the cave to seek the Lord, the enemies goes back with a testimony of how great is our God.

King Saul went back with a testimony and acknowledged that David will be a

> "Our destiny changes with our thought; we shall become what we wish to become, do what we wish to do, when our habitual thought corresponds with our desire."
>
> - *Orison Swett Marden*

king (1 Sam 24:20). The reason why many fail in their spiritual walk, is perhaps lack of knowledge on the cave to hide during tough times. David's secret of success when fighting his enemies was hiding in the cave of Adullum which means, 'justice of the people'.

> "It isn't where you came from; it's where you're going that counts."
>
> — *Ella Fitzgerald*

Despite, the fact that he had done nothing wrong to Saul c.f 1 Sam 20:1, who was after his life, God administered justice in Adullum. May the Lord help us acknowledge the cave of Justice whenever we reach to the end! God is always a stronghold even when he seems absent, his presence is still inevitable. He is both transcendent and immanent. Transcendent means that God exists far above, independent of His creation. Immanence is the literal meaning 'to be 'within' or 'near' His creation.

Rev Antony Kimani Nganga

Lot's potential was limited within the confines of the cave. There is no record of an innovation by Lot when he lived in the cave. His ability to think and discover his potential was minimal. This was so because he couldn't travel and interact with the world outside the cave.

Just like lot, there are many individuals who never leave their comfort zones to explore the world. They have become a 'cave men' living in a cocoon of potential slavery, who mostly agree with the people who thinks and walk their talk. They never wrestle with their established brain connections by trying something new to taking a different route to work. Exposure is nothing but coming out the cocoon to discover the unlimited potential.

The man Moses was exposed such that he challenged the world of the day with his leadership abilities. We are told by the gospel according to Acts17:22, how he was learned in all the wisdom of Egyptians and became powerful in speech and in action. Apostle Paul, became all things to all men so that by all possible means he might save some (1 Cor. 9:22).

He also realized that a call to ministry is a call to preparation by learning the Hebrew law under Gamaliel who was an expert in the religious law (Acts 5:34). Apart from Christ, there has never been a missionary who have accomplished much more than the Apostle Paul.

Today, we see a majority of spiritual leaders hindering opportunities where spiritual gifts of the young generation can grow. This has happened to most of our youths in the community. Whenever someone rises up in the community with phenomenal abilities, 'older spiritual folks' are there to discourage. It's also evident in most Kenyan societies and churches in particular. One time we ministered in a

> "Everybody's got the potential for great good and great wrong in them, but it's the choices we make that define who we really are."
>
> — *Charles de Lint*

fellowship during a college internship at Pentecostal church, after being there for over nine months. The members went spreading the powerful message for a couple of days. The Local Church minister ensured that I never appeared again in the preaching program. He couldn't believe in anyone preaching 'powerfully' more than he did. Fortunately, God opened another door. I got invitations from other churches, colleges and Universities, such that I had to gather a team who ministered together with me.

Later, I joined another fellowship where God dealt with me at a different level. You will never graduate to the next level until you discover what God has in store for you. Whenever God equips you for a task, never settle down for anything less other than for fulfilling it.

Oprah Winfrey was fired from her first television job as an anchor in Baltimore, where she said she faced sexism and harassment. But Winfrey rebounded and became the undisputed queen of television talk shows before amassing a media empire. Today she is worth an estimated $2.9 billion, according to Forbes. Failure was not a stumbling block to her success in life. Instead, it was a stepping stone for greater opportunities. Most of us today, may be victims of circumstances like Oprah. But we can learn to recognize that failure is not final and keep moving. Martin Luther King Junior once said, 'if you can't fly, run; if you can't run, walk; if you can't walk crawl, but by all means keep moving.

Thomas Edison's teachers told him he was "too stupid to learn anything." But Thomas Edison had a different spirit of looking at it. He believed in living to what God had destined him to be. This is evident by the fact that he went on to hold more than 1,000 patents and invented some world-changing devices, like the phonograph, practical electrical lamp, and a movie camera.

> "There is no planet, sun, or star could hold you if you but knew what you are."
>
> — *Ralph Waldo Emerson*

The moment we discover our purpose for existence, let's rise for it. We are able to shift your focus from our past with the devil to our future with Jesus. Whenever the devil reminds us of our past, remind him of his future in the lake of fire. The past will always hold us captive to our destiny. Never allow others intimidate you based on your past, but keep on moving towards your goals.

No matter how slow you may walk, ensure you live to fulfill God's purpose in your life. There's nothing that can stop any individual from becoming the person God designed them to be. It's only the individual that can interrupt their destiny, not God. God created human beings with all that it takes to succeed in life.

He says in Isaiah 54:17, *'no weapon forged against you will prevail, and you will refute every tongue that accuses you. This is the heritage of the servants of the LORD, and this is their vindication from me," declares the LORD* (NIV).' The Lord has given us his word as a guide. The word heritage used in this context means 'inheritance'. An inheritance is not like a gift or a reward, it's a birthright.

Rev Antony Kimani Nganga

# 8

# Divine Guidance

# is All

# You Need!

Rev Antony Kimani Nganga

**8**

## Divine guidance is all you need!

*"There's no 'ifs' in God's world. And no places that are safer than other places. The center of his will is our only safety – let us pray that we may always know it!"*

**____Corrie ten Boom____**

In Gen 19:26, we see the wife of Lot becoming a pillar of salt after looking back. God will never compromise with his decrees even when we do. Even when we give up on the way and think on turning back, He still remains faithful in the process.

We can't choose to follow both God and our thoughts the same time. We may not end up being where God want us to be, if rely on the past like the wife of Lot. Heb. 12:1 *'says therefore, since we are surrounded by such a great cloud of witnesses, we must get rid of every weight and the sin that clings so closely, and run with endurance the race set out for us,'* (NET)

Rev Antony Kimani Nganga

In Genesis 13, we see both Lot and Abram as rich men. There was strife between Lot's and Abram herdsmen in charge of their livestock. Abram told Lot to choose his portion to avoid strife. We are told in verse 10, that Lot chose himself the whole Jordan plain that was well watered like the garden of the Lord.

When Lot moved Sodom, the Lord appeared to Abram and promised to bless him and his

> "You've been given the innate power to shape your life."
>
> — *Steve Maraboli*

descendants forever. Abram was blessed of the Lord! Sometimes for God to bless us, we need to get rid of some people from our lives. Get rid of the wrong company that doesn't add value in your life. Until we realize these truths, we'll remain stuck in living our dreams and goals in life.

How many times do we miss the blessings of the Lord by following our own finite minds? As Christians, before we make any decisions it's important to consult God (Prov. 3:5-7). The best advice is from above!

Lots concept of success was based on materialism. It's perplexing to know how many friends we have in life just because of what we have and not for who we are. As long they get something from us, they will pretend by all means to be our friend. We need to face such stereotype kind of friends and tell them enough is enough! In fact, the scriptures warn us that a man with many friends can be ruined (Prov. 18:24)

"Don't entrust your future on others' hands. Rather make decisions by yourself with the help of God's guidance. Hold your beliefs so tight and never let go of them!"

— *Hark Herald Sarmiento*

Most young adults in the United States are stuck in a quagmire and looking for help. A significant number of young adults holds to the ideology that, for a girl to be engaged a man has to buy the ring of her choice.

Most of those rings are very costly. That reflects absolute materialism that's probably rooted in pride or even egocentric motives.

We need to realize who we are is more important that what we have. If a girl's motive for marriage is to gain wealth, she miss it! You don't marry a rich person for material gains. This is simply because, success is not sexually transmitted. A wealthy partner should always be seen as an added advantage.

It's better to establish a relationship with the God of the girls because when you have God, you have all you need! Materialism cannot work under this principle. God leads those that honestly seeks divine guidance.

I have always allowed God to direct my thoughts in choosing my future mate. Matthew 6:3 puts it clearly *'But seek ye first the kingdom of God, and his righteousness; and all these things shall be added unto you'* (KJV) Most individuals want vice versa. They want the girls of God rather than the God of the girls. Seeking the blessings of God and God of the blessings. We commit ourselves to the program of God and forget the God of the program. Due to this attitude, many have been left doing the programs of God without personal experience with God

> "Never pray to be a better slave when God is trying to get you out of your situation."
>
> — *Shannon L. Alder*

who transforms the life of an individual. When transformation is absent; secularism, legalism, and Hollywood practices are inevitable.

Christian maturity is not and will never be spiritual maturity. You can grow old and still remain a baby in your spiritual walk. Maturity is not a matter of age, its acceptance of responsibility. God does not deal with us on what we do. Neither does He deal with where we come from but on who we are. Who we are is more important to God than what we do in His kingdom.

It's not what we give to God that activates his love in our lives. There's nothing we can do to draw God in our lives. Actually, we can't give to God no matter how we give. Only those who recognize this fact demonstrates his manifestations in their spiritual walk. It is the high time the church needs to realize her purpose and demonstrate the same.

Lot neglected divine guidance before he got in the cave and also when he lived there. Divine guidance leads us to know the will of God in our lives. Moses knew the secret of Divine guidance as He says to God that they can't go unless His presence goes with them (Ex. 33:15). If we can't allow God to guide our thoughts certainly, the devil will. Satan acts an opportunist by misleading us to sin.

Unfortunately, we may end up making the wrong decisions if we seek advice from the wrong people. It's impossible to make proper choices in life based on right counsel from above. That's why some mess up and even end up with regrets and pain in their hearts as a result. David in Psalms 23: 1 said, *"The Lord is my shepherd..."* This was an expression of how God walked with him in difficult times. Any individual determined to reach their destiny need to appreciate the impact of divine guidance in their lives.

> "The right thing at the wrong tme is the wrong thing."
>
> — *Joshua Harris*

When I departed my Kenya for further studies abroad, my fellow immigrants in the state Georgia gave a lot of counsel. I remember some expressing how pathetic my situation was. I grieved in my heart, considering how a friend can give such a weird advice and I was not even in need of any advice. But acknowledging the fact that, am on a mission in the United States, I purposed to pursue my goals in the midst of challenges. The Holy Scriptures, especially Philippians 1:6 had a deeper meaning whenever I felt subscribing to the opinion of others. I knew the one who started the good work in me is faithful and will perfect it until the day of Christ Jesus.

# 9

# Challenges

# in the

# Foreign Land

Rev Antony Kimani Nganga

## Challenges in the foreign land

*'The best years of your life are the ones in which your problems are your own. You do not blame them on your mother, the ecology, or the president. You realize that you control your own destiny"*

_____*Albert Ellis*_____

It is often told that every person has a story to tell. The passion that ignites the desire to put my story in this book is to encourage all called servants of God. I conquer with the Kenyan female actress Lupita Nyong'o, and the 2014 Oscars award winner, when she said 'no matter where you are from, your dreams are valid.'

In pursuit of excellence, my journey to the United States started in a vision on a mission at a local High school the year 2010. I was in a *'matatu'* which is a local name for a public transport vehicle and had no fare to pay for the service. A lady in the matatu, looked at the back and happened to recognize me. She told me that she has paid my fare and prophesied that I will travel overseas to preach the gospel. This was not real to me until God used another servant of God, Pst Evans Wamagata at a youth conference held in Kenya P.E.F.A Church.

This was the year I had enrolled at Nairobi Pentecostal Bible College in Garden Estate, Nairobi. Most High schools sent invitations to preach on Sundays and impact biblical truths. As I was praying for 76 students at Kijabe girls in a Sunday service, God took me in the spirit and showed me as being a student at Beulah Heights University. I didn't hesitate rather, I went ahead and sent an email to the director of admissions who was Mr. John Dreher and explained to him how the Lord is leading me on the same.

I had no idea about the fax, FedEx, or even DHL, as a fast and convenient way of sending official documents to the school. The only thing I knew was to send letters using local postage. Since, this was the only available means of sending my documents to the school, I sent my application materials thrice without success. This process took me almost two years, but I still had the conviction to press on. This period I learnt that, Persistence wears out resistance!

On July 2013, I decided to give up and possibly try a different school since; I had graduated with a Diploma in Bible and Theology and the need to further my studies. I decided to send an email to the director of admissions with the intent of giving up on the process. This time it was Mrs. Dudley who was newly appointed as the director of admissions. She sympathized with my situation and encouraged me to email the scan copies of my documents. She helped through together with Arthur Breland and within three weeks, I had received the official acceptance documents.

Two years of seeking admissions at Beulah Heights taught me patience and long-suffering. This was a time of preparation as God exposed me in a multicultural and advanced world where His calling would be challenged. It was a moment in my life where, I was in darkness not knowing where God wants me to go. I have learned to trust God even when He seems to hide and invisible.

> "God intentionally allows you to go through painful experiences to equip you for ministry to others."
>
> — Rick Warren

My folks believes in supporting the call of God in my life. They had gone with me through thick and thin. Since it was a school policy for international students to deposit $3000 in order to receive official acceptance documents. They had to sell their land located in Kenya and also get a loan from Equity bank of Kenya to pay the deposit.

Since, it was our first time to send money through the western union I had to keep on asking if the money was received at the school. The deposit was enough to pay air ticket as well as buy some few clothes.

A day before leaving to the United States, we invited friends and relatives for a farewell banquet. Most of my friends came to bid me farewell. But some started fighting for the beautiful girls after being energized by the meal. Moreover, they even damaged some house items. I felt bad when I realized they were my very close friends. But I prayed God to help me handle the situation without anger and bitterness.

**"Affliction is a good man's shining time."**

*— Edward Young*

I landed in Atlanta, Georgia during the winter season. I had only one sweater that couldn't keep me warm. Fortunately, a Pastor in Lakewood Terrace bought me a heavier coat to keep me warm. I had to report school for classes on this inclement weather. Since, I only had $300 in my pocket I bought a pedal bike at US$110 for riding to school.

I reported to school riding on a bike when it

was $10^{O}$F in the morning. When the Registrar saw me, he went for his heavy coat in the car and gave it to me. I remember he kept on telling me 'This is crazy'. I told him my purpose is getting to school no matter how low the temperature gets. He sympathized with me so much. He informed the college president, Dr. Benson Karanja of a 'crazy man' from Kenya who came riding on a pedal bike in the freezing weather.

The following day, the president gave me his clothes and requested others to do the same. I remember my Literature professor; Dr. Angelissa Cummings giving me two beautiful sweaters, I felt loved and cared for.

The weather could get to freezing rates and would be deadly for me to ride the bike. I remember riding the bike from school when temperatures went as low as $8^{o}$F or $-13.3^{o}$c. I rang my roommate to pick me quickly down the street before am frozen. I thank God for saving me that day.

The greatest achievers say that, in a lifetime of setbacks and comebacks, the truest sense of accomplishment is not found in the realization of the goal, but rather in the will to continue when failure breeds doubt. Eventually, I landed in the hands of Dr. Chris Bowen who believed that I can succeed no matter how pathetic my situation seemed to be. He is an icon in the lives of many as God uses him in extra-ordinary ways to walk with people to their destiny.

He gave me a laptop after acknowledging my passion in writing. He spent many days mentoring and motivating me for the best. I remember how he spent his valuable time taking me out especially for lunch. He stood with me all through and I respect him for that together with his family and Living faith Tabernacle, Forest park, Georgia USA.

On the month of August, I was given thirty days' notice to leave the house since I wasn't able to keep up with the bills. I had nowhere to go. But before thirty days were over, I requested for an extension for one more week. Before seven days were over, God went someone on the fourth day with a job offer. I may not be where God wants me to be, but I thank Him that am no longer where I used to be. God has proved himself faithful in my life, just as He promises in His word. We serve a faithful God who answers prayers!

I have always wanted to be a minister, and today am a licensed clergyman. I have always wanted to be an author, today am a published writer. I have always wanted to be a renowned motivational speaker, today am one of the youngest motivational speaker in North America and parts of Africa. All that I have been dreaming, my eyes have seen the coming of the glory of the Lord. I have always to plant a tree, I have a grove of them. Last but not the least, raising a kid is the assignment am about to undertake. If God has been faithful this far, I will continuously focus unto Him than ever before.

All that have transpired in my life is worth concluding with Steve Jobs advice that 'Sometimes life hits you in the head with a brick. Don't lose faith.

I am convinced that the only thing that kept me going was loving what I did.

You've got to find what you love. And that is as true for your work as it is for your lovers. Your work is going to fill a large part of your life, and the only way to be truly satisfied is to do what you believe is great work.

And the only way to do great work is to love what you do. If you haven't found it yet, keep looking. Don't settle. As with all matters of the heart, you'll know when you find it. And, like any great relationship, it just gets better and better as the years roll on. So keep looking until you find it. Don't settle.

Your time is limited, so don't waste it living someone else's life. Don't be trapped by dogma- which is living with the results of other people's thinking. Don't let other people's opinions put you down! And most important, have the courage to follow your heart and intuition. They somehow already know what you truly want to become. Everything else is secondary'.

Rev Antony Kimani Nganga

# 10

# The Woman

# on Purpose

Rev Antony Kimani Nganga

**10**

**The woman on Purpose**

*'But his wife looked back from behind him, and she became a pillar of salt.'* **Gen 19:26**

"Healthy relationships should always begin at the spiritual and intellectual levels - the levels of purpose, dreams, motivation, interests, and personality."

*-Myles Munroe,*

We live in a complex society with both negative and positive influences. The impact of individuals and their relationships, such as the mass media, the internet, changing gender roles and growing urban crowding. This has challenged the modern world in shaping the ideal wife.

The wife of Lot doesn't represent a model of a woman on purpose. She demonstrates the Character of unwillingness in making the right decisions that would have eventually shaped her destiny. She was not interested in moving the same direction with the husband and therefore, faced the wrath of God.

Reinforcing this, James 1:8 says, a double minded man is unstable in all his ways. Most marriage suffers because of such reflections of character qualities. If one gets in marriage with an intention of trying to see if it works, the possibility for such a marriage to work are minimal.

> "Define success on your own terms, achieve it by your own rules, and build a life you're proud to live."
>
> **Anne Sweeney**

Marriage is the only school one is awarded a certificate the first day and there are no drop-outs. The wife of Lot however decided to drop-out by visualizing on the wicked territory of Sodom.

In the Bible, there are women who got to their destiny by demonstrating a greater faith than that of their husbands. Elizabeth, the mother of John the

Baptist is one among the few. The word Elizabeth means "God's promise" or "God is generous." The Bible says in Luke 1:7, that Elizabeth was barren! When the angel of the Lord told Zachariah that his wife would conceive, he did not believe and was thus struck dumb but Elizabeth had no problem believing. Zechariah became a dumb man from the time the angel appeared to him until the child was born. Sometimes God closes the mouth of our loved ones for a miracle to happen and his purpose to prevail.

Unfortunately, that the ideal wife is a rare commodity especially in the African-American

> "You may not always have a comfortable life and you will not always be able to solve all of the world's problems at once but don't ever underestimate the importance you can have because history has shown us that courage can be contagious and hope can take on a life of its own."
>
> *—Michelle Obama*

Community. Most of us has allowed secular marriage concepts and practices redefine the biblical concept that we claim to stand for. We must not be ignorant of the negative impact of

> "Not all of us can do great things. But we can do small things with great love."
>
> **– Mother Teresa**

our environment that leaves our minds stained.

There are 21st Century women who have gone through severe pain, hurts and hardships yet they remained focused to their destiny. Kakenya Ntaiya from Enoosaen, a small Maasai village in Western Kenya is a good example. When she was 14 years old, Kakenya entered the cow pen behind her homestead with an elderly woman carrying a rusty knife. In the presence of other villagers, she was mutilated. Since one is not expected to cry due to pain, she fainted on the ground.

Today, female genital mutilation is illegal in Kenya, but education for the girl child has not been a priority in Maasai culture. However, she was able to overcome the tradition of the day by excelling in her studies and earned a college scholarship in the United States. She promised her community to return and help the village. She came to the United States with an assignment of breaking evil traditions when upon her return.

She opened the first primary school for girls in her village, the Kakenya Center of Excellence in 2009. Today, Ntaiya is helping more than 200 girls receive the education and other opportunities that she struggled so much to achieve. The school has helped young girls from being sexually assaulted as they don't have to walk miles back and forth.

> "I learned to always take on things I'd never done before. Growth and comfort do not coexist."
> - *Virginia Rometty*
> *(CEO of IBM)*

Mother Teresa (1910-1997) is a model of selfless commitment throughout history. He devoted her life to the service of the poor and selfless service to others around the globe. She cared for thousands of sick and dying in Calcutta. Due to this, she was honored with a Nobel Peace Prize award in 1979.

The ideal wife is focused on the subject more than the object. The wife of Lot was reflected interest of being in Sodom more than in following God. She had her focus on the mortal rather than the immortal. Most of the wives that subscribe to this concept ends up in confusion and regrets. The moment she looked back, she disconnected herself from divine destiny.

The ideal wife recognizes her marriage is

"Passion is energy. Feel the power that comes from focusing on what excites you."
– *Oprah Winfrey*

built on God's promises not material possessions. It is true that most ladies will have great appetite for material possessions. But the problem is when your interests outdo the purpose for which marriage is meant. Many are deceived with what they see with their eyes. Lot was a rich man when he lived with Abraham, but he lost his property in Sodom. It's assumed that the wife of Lot was recalling their wealth left in Sodom. As a result, God struck her to death. This was a double tragedy; she lost her life and the husband by acting contrary to God's will.

> **"As a leader, I am tough on myself and I raise the standard for everybody; however, I am very caring because I want people to excel at what they are doing so that they can aspire to be me in the future."**
>
> **- Indra Nooyi**
>
> **(CEO of *PepsiCo*)**

The ideal wife has a vision for her family. She doesn't get in marriage simply because of finding Mr. Right. For instance, at a youth conference in Kenya, a lady came to me with a list of traits she was looking for in a man. She gave it to me as a prayer request. The list was long and filled with descriptions of the imaginable future husband. But after scanning her list, I told her "you don't need a husband, you need Jesus". I told her that the description of that person is none other than Jesus. She gave her life to Jesus, and became a light and a witness to many. I believe it's not so much finding the right person, but being the right person that counts in marriage.

If you want a queen, you need to be a king. If you need a good lover, you need to be a good lover. If you are looking for lover, you must demonstrate and live it.

"I've learned that people will forget what you said, people will forget what you did, but people will never forget how you made them feel."

– *Maya Angelou*

GIRLFRIEND V/S WIFE

Wife is Like a TV; Girlfriend is Like a MOBILE

At home you watch TV, but when you go out, you take your MOBILE.

No money, you sell the TV, got money you change your MOBILE.

Sometimes you enjoy TV, but most of the time you play with your MOBILE.

TV is free for life, but for the MOBILE, if you don't pay, the services will be terminated. That is the relationship.

TV is big, bulky and most of the time old!

But the MOBILE is cute, slim, curvy and very portable.

Operational costs for TV is often acceptable, but for the MOBILE it is often high and demanding.

TV has a remote, MOBILE doesn't.

You watch the TV from a distance, the MOBILE is always in contact with your body during communication, close to the mouth and the ear while you hold it with your hands. It's something you really love. The TV can never keep secrets. When it talks, everybody in the room listens.

When the MOBILE talks the communication is secret.

You can never send the TV a secret message but with your MOBILE, you can send an SMS, very secret indeed.

Once you leave home, the TV is out of mind. Once the TV is out of mind, your MOBILE takes over and keeps you company.

If you forget your MOBILE, you return to fetch it if possible because it is always much closer to your heart.

MOBILE is a two-way communication (you talk and listen), but with the TV you

MUST only listen (whether you want to or not).

The TV never learns new tricks of the game and has never helped you go online. It is old fashioned.

Your MOBILE went online long time and even

enables you to send/receive photos and play MP3s. It's more fashionable!

Most Importantly: TVs don't have viruses but MOBILES often do…It's cute but dangerous!

In any case, the initials "TV" stands for "Too Vague" for comfort.

"MOBILE" stands for "My Obedient Babie Is Lovable Eternally". You will never do without it!

Retrieved from http://kenyastockholm.com/2011/02/09/reader-request-wife-is-like-a-tv-girlfriend-is-like-a-mobile/

Rev Antony Kimani Nganga

Rev Antony Kimani Nganga

Made in the USA
Charleston, SC
15 April 2015